UNDERWATER COUNTING

COUNTING

Even Numbers

Jerry Pallotta

David Biedrzycki

Charlesbridge

Thank you to Suzanne Norgren, Shirley Stahl, Karen Kellog, Jane Miller,
Ann Tuteur, Jane Yearout, Linda Brooks, Marlene Malkin, Pat Crawford, and Clare Bursky.
—J. P.

To my sister, Lois, the accountant. You've always had my number.
—D. B.

Published by Charlesbridge Publishing
85 Main Street, Watertown, MA 02472
(617) 926-0329
www.charlesbridge.com

Illustrations in this book done in Adobe Photoshop
Text type set in Cochin
Color separations by Sung In Printing, South Korea
Printed and bound by Sung In Printing, South Korea

Library of Congress Cataloging-in-Publication Data
Available upon request.

ISBN 0-88106-952-3 (reinforced for library use)
ISBN 0-88106-800-4 (softcover)

Printed in South Korea
(hc) 10 9 8 7 6 5 4 3
(sc) 10 9 8 7 6 5 4 3

Books by Jerry Pallotta:
The Icky Bug Alphabet Book
The Icky Bug Alphabet Board Book
The Bird Alphabet Book
The Ocean Alphabet Book
The Flower Alphabet Book
The Yucky Reptile Alphabet Book
The Frog Alphabet Book
The Furry Animal Alphabet Book
The Dinosaur Alphabet Book
The Underwater Alphabet Book
The Victory Garden Vegetable Alphabet Book
The Extinct Alphabet Book
The Desert Alphabet Book
The Spice Alphabet Book
The Butterfly Alphabet Book
The Freshwater Alphabet Book
The Airplane Alphabet Book
The Boat Alphabet Book
The Jet Alphabet Book
Going Lobstering
Dory Story
The Icky Bug Counting Book
Cuenta los insectos (The Icky Bug Counting Book)
The Crayon Counting Book
The Crayon Counting Board Book

There are zero fish swimming on this page.
Maybe they were chased away by a shark.
Or maybe you scared them off when
you opened this book!

0
zero

Here is one Green Moray Eel. These fish really have blue skin. They look green because they have yellow slime all over their bodies. Blue plus yellow equals green!

Hmm . . . maybe it's too easy to count by ones. Let's count by even numbers instead.

Here are two Coral Groupers.
If you were this fish, people
would say you had measles,
chicken pox, or really
cute freckles.

These four Clown Triggerfish are odd looking. While counting, please remember that whole numbers ending in one, three, five, seven, and nine are odd numbers. Even numbers end in zero, two, four, six, and eight.

4
four

Count the six Manta Rays. It's hard to believe how large they are. They weigh up to three thousand pounds—a ton and a half! From wing tip to wing tip, each can be as wide as three elephants.

6

six

8
eight

Billfish are species of fish that have long, sword-like noses. These eight Sailfish are a type of billfish.

Sailfish can swim up to seventy miles per hour. That's fast! Their huge, sail-like fins allow them to make sharp turns at full speed.

10
ten

These ten Harlequin Tuskfish have bright blue teeth. Would you like to have blue teeth?

12
twelve

Notice the bright spots below the eyes of these twelve Flashlight Fish. The light actually comes from glow-in-the-dark bacteria that live on the fish. Batteries not included!

14
fourteen

Flyingfish are a welcome sight for hungry sailors far from land or lost at sea. Who needs to go fishing? Flyingfish have been known to land right on deck or in a life raft.

These fish don't fly in the sky like birds. However, they can glide over the ocean, some for the length of a soccer field. Don't forget to count to fourteen!

16
sixteen

Crunch! Crunch! If you go diving on a reef and see bite marks on the coral, they were probably made by a Parrotfish. Parrotfish have fused teeth that look like a beak. Their teeth are perfect for crunching on hard coral. Here are sixteen Parrotfish.

These eighteen weird-looking fish have multiple names. They can be called Pineapple Fish, Pinecone Fish, or Knight Fish. They look like a pineapple, feel like a pinecone, and are spiked and armored like a medieval knight.

18
eighteen

20 twenty

Count the twenty Trumpetfish. They swim like other fish, but when they want to hide in coral and seaweed, they hover vertically. If these fish could read, this is how they would place the type.

A group of birds is called a flock. A group of wolves is called a pack. A group of fish is called a school. You twenty-two Achilles Tangs, stay in school!

Here's a school of twenty-four
Señoritas. When you see a school of fish,
the fish in it are always the same size and
species. Adult fish don't school with the young,
and the young don't school with the adults.

Do these twenty-six Whale Lice gross you out? Whales sometimes have lice. These tiny crustaceans hook a ride on the whale and live on its skin.

26
twenty-six

28
twenty-eight

Sharks have a deadly reputation, but it is mostly undeserved. More people die each year from dog attacks than from shark attacks. These twenty-eight Leopard Sharks get their name from the pretty spots on their skin.

Look closely. The sneaky illustrator
played a trick on your eyes. . . .

You can count the thirty Lemonpeels, but it
would also be fun to learn the names of all the
different fins on a fish. The caudal fin is on the tail,
the dorsal fin is on the back, the pectoral fins are on the
sides near the gills, the anal fin is on the bottom near the
tail, and the pelvic fins are on the bottom closer to the head.

32
thirty-two

Let's go back in time!
Pretend that all of a sudden it's
one hundred and fifty million years ago.
There are fish in the ocean, but the ones on
the other pages of this book are not around yet.

Back then, dinosaurs walked on land, pterosaurs flew in the
sky, and plesiosaurs swam in the ocean. These thirty-two
Elasmosaurs are a type of plesiosaur, an ocean reptile.

Obviously this fish gets its name from the math game
of dominoes. While you're counting the thirty-four
Domino Damselfish, you'll notice that none of
them have eyelids. Like all fish, they keep
their eyes open all the time, even when
they take a rest or go to sleep.

34
thirty-four

These thirty-six Squirrelfish are easy to
recognize. During the day they squirrel themselves
into little hidden crevices. At night, it's dinnertime!
Their big eyes help them feed in the dark.

Something doesn't look right. What are these thirty-eight fish? Lookdowns! Their huge foreheads, high eyes, and low mouths make it seem like they are looking down.

38

thirty-eight

Count the forty Bird-nosed Wrasses. These fish have long snouts, like anteaters. Their mouths are perfectly shaped for finding food in hard-to-reach places. Too bad there are no ants in the ocean.

40
forty

42

forty-two

Like all other jellyfish, these forty-two Moon Jellies swim at the mercy of the sea. If a jellyfish washes up on shore and the hot sun dries it out, hardly anything is left of it. Jellyfish are ninety-five percent water.

Run, turtles, run! Run as fast as you can! Watch out for hungry crabs and sea birds! Then swim, swim as fast as you can! Watch out for sharks and other turtle-eating fish!

Once these forty-four Green Sea Turtles make their mad dash for the ocean, they will swim for up to twenty-four hours straight before resting. Very few of these baby turtles will live to become adults.

44

forty-four

If you go swimming near these forty-six
Barracudas, do not wear a watch or jewelry.
Barracudas dart after shiny objects. They
usually feed by sight,
not by smell.

These fish really get around! Hundreds of species of Gobies swim in all the world's oceans, except for the freezing cold Arctic and Antarctic Oceans. Some Gobies even live in fresh water. Here are forty-eight Fire Gobies. On to fifty!

50
fifty

We end this book with fifty Fishing Bats. Fishing isn't just for people. These bats sense a change in the surface of the ocean, and then they swoop down and catch their supper.

So sorry, Señorita!